I0625555

Be Still Mere Molecule

Be Still Mere Molecule

Poems

Rebecca A. Durham

BROKEN TRIBE PRESS

Be Still Mere Molecule is the 2024 Winner of the Tribe Poetry Award

Be Still Mere Molecule

Copyright © 2025 Rebecca A. Durham
First Edition

Paperback ISBN: 978-1-965412-10-7

Library of Congress Control Number: 2025902174

All rights reserved. No part of this book may be reproduced or transmitted in any form or by any means, electronic, digital, or mechanical, including photocopy, audio recording, or any information storage and retrieval system, without prior permission from the publisher or author (except by reviewers who may quote brief passages).

Cover art by Rebecca A. Durham
Author photo by Emaline Aspen

Cover design by Jacob Arms

Published by Broken Tribe Press
Lawrence Landing Company
Raleigh, North Carolina 27609
USA, North America

Broken Tribe Press is a proud member of:

Independent Book Publishers Association
 and
Community of Literary Magazines and Presses

www.brokentribepress.com

BROKEN TRIBE PRESS

ADVANCE PRAISE

Be Still Mere Molecule draws us in in jubilation, in the squishy ecstasy of emergence: "fallen/bodies/tumble into connection/sedges cloak the muck/step in, step in" – and we do! Seducing with 'mycelial language,' this deeply grounded collection invites us to go on a field trip with a luxuriant botanist who sings plant names into a 'web of nurture.' Here's a weft of pain/breath, the luster of a pearl's lacquer, pleading birds, quartz cliffs refracting the spark-sheen. Rebecca Durham calls to the tendrils in a deep ecopoetic symphony, and they respond in glory: "You rise to cultivate these green galaxies/like rootlets sprung from a stellar maze."

—Petra Kuppers, author of *Eco Soma* and *Diver Beneath the Street*

Rebecca Durham's most recent collection of poems, *Be Still Mere Molecule*, is a wonder. Durham is equal parts poet and scientist. The speaker is an observer of emotional depth, profoundly engaged with the physical world. The scientist observes and names. The poet, attuned to sensory and tonal connections, understands how the shepherding of sound can create unique subliminal tones. The poet hears the musicality intrinsic to the language of science. Nomenclature becomes a concordance of cadence. She shares a world that few of us have the vocabulary or knowledge to travel on our own. Durham wants to share with us how she sees our world. Take a walk with Rebecca Durham. Let her share the world she is discovering.

—Gerald Wagoner, author of *When Nothing Wild Remains* and *A Month of Someday*

Be Still Mere Molecule is a deep and joyful exploration of the natural sciences prismed through the lens of poetry. Using her extensive knowledge of botany and ecology, Durham deftly integrates scientific terms, equations, and chemical structures in her poems, creating a rich "mycelial language" that binds concepts and processes from nature with themes of wonder, longing, and environmental loss. Durham speaks with scientific precision and emotional urgency about environmental threats as she chronicles the "blind hum of hostile elements" in the human body or how "the golden-crowned kinglet collides with glass". Yet, this collection is also "a chant for wholeness" permeated by enduring beauty and resilience as Durham reminds us "at long last the ice recedes / and the first bird-wakes ripple the open water" and how "joy must be self-taught / again and again, continuous."

—Laurel Anderson, plant ecologist and poet

To my mother, Judith Clayton Durham,
for her steadfast encouragement of my creative and scientific pursuits.

Contents

ECOLOGY

Rootlets Push   1

Knowing is a kind of prayer   2

The Ecological Implications Are Considered   3

April 17, 2023, 48.498337°, -114.437207°   4

Desire unspools like green globe chains   6

Two Fungal Species Among Many Play Telephone and Ferret Food   7

Press Down to be Amazed   8

Asterisks Indicate Significant Differences   9

Foraging Behavior of the Wood-rotting Fungus   10

BIOLOGY

How We See Photons' Slight Glimmer   13

We take the rotary ride   16

Evolved to Make Metabolic Sense   17

Ensnaring The Pain Burden   18

To travel arteriorly   23

Mother of Pearl, or One of the Manifestations   24

ORNITHOLOGY

Brindle Brown   31

When Birds Drink Seawater Salt Moves Through Their
    Blood Into Salt Glands And Out Of Their Bodies   32

White Horizon Over Black-Green Woods   33

A Museum of Bohemian Waxwings, March 5th   34

Go Away, It's Spring   35

You Can Tell It's a Mountain Chickadee
    By The White Stripe Above the Eye   36

I hear how calendula petals   37

BOTANY

Merry Quotidian   41

Arise All Tendrils   42

Tatters tore at the people   43

Is it a Plant Feedback Loop   44

Potential Additional Research   45

Consider the Plant's Perspective   46

Why Not Inhabit Sunlight?   47

Study of Achenes   48

ASTRONOMY & ATMOSPHERIC SCIENCE

Ramping Up   53

Altocumulus lenticularis   55

Grief, unlike stars   56

Cold mountain feeling   57

Completely Blocked by the Occluding Body   58

Space Just Landed   59

GEOLOGY

Please Provide Proof of Universal Schism   63

Gneiss of the Cascades Core or O Orogenesis   64

Quartz Cliffs Not Broken by Rime   67

PHYSICS & MATH

Nor Could the Sun   71

Show How It Might Be So   72

The heart refuses circumference   74

Be Still, Mere Molecule   75

There Will Be Harmonies   76

If We Change the Same Set of Basic Physics Equations   78

CHEMISTRY

Wood Parade   81

Marginalia on The Table of Elements Including
   Names, Symbols, and Atomic Numbers   82

It would be just like you, universe   84

Ki is a smoke wisp & I   85

And In This Regard We Breathe Shapes   86

ENVIRONMENTAL SCIENCE

I dream we are Anthropocene torture machines   91

Heavy Metal Hangover   92

Ashes Again   93

Keep Your Hands Inside the Anthropocene at All Times   94

Mercury Lurks in My Milk Chocolate   95

I Heard Seawater is Blood Kin   96

Look at This Bliss   98

Acknowledgements   99

Notes   100

References   103

ECOLOGY

Rootlets Push

into the deep duff of it

organic matter dank with richness

dark soil woven by hyphae

a mirth of light on mosses

a chant for wholeness

hermit thrush led

where do

we keep fallen

bodies

tumble into connection

sedges cloak the muck

step in, step in

Knowing is a kind of prayer

that tumbles open a belonging
built with mycelial language.

That feathered geometry
ferreting food and words
not letters but carbon rings
and elements.

Bonds cling and cleave along the web
sugar excretion, uptake, catabolism, anabolism—
          vast linkages surge while I linger.

I touch *Cladonia* lichen
the grey-green pixie cups
and mint shreds of squamules that fill
the gaps between the vascular plants
of the understory, which is also a story.

I am a kind of story, too
a planter, a keeper, a craver of fractals,
kisser of wilderness.

The trees generosity, fanning out
in cryptic constellations
          eludes us   as we make our crude maps—
                ions cascade and build
                encircle root tendrils.

Fungi exudes acids and enzymes
  spores rain   windborne
        like the achenes of *Agoseris*
          whose capillary wisps   dehisce
              pirouette and fall

alight on moss-cradled cedars

sow-scattered

cultivated from my breath-wind
        exalted.

The Ecological Implications Are Considered

In summary   how intricate
Our results suggest   the intertwined cling
Linkages   innumerable linkages
That may be dependent   so we gather near these lines
That have been demonstrated   and it will go on from there
That may require   each connection
Maximum retention   holds fast to the other
Thus, may be   it goes on from there
Especially desirable   honoring what is held

April 17, 2023, 48.498337°, -114.437207°

The ground has been spring cleaned; rain freshened from the flattening.
Green springs up from rosettes past, edges still snow-stung and browned.

Arisen: Arnica leaves open to each other and hugging, Bluebell leaves
rotund and upright in an eager bunch, Skunk Cabbage sun-yellow

spadix and spathe; green Strawberry leaflets unfolding as an accordion,
Yarrow's feathered-cut leaves radiating out like a Fibonacci spiral. Subtler

still is Huckleberry who just breached crimson budscales, and above the
early spring scene waves Usnea and Bryoria, who all the while have waited

for someone to stir, as there had not been much to watch below, with all
that monochrome cover as hovers winter. Across the path, Larch needles

caught mid-splendor by the final wind scour create a Sphagnum-like
landing and each step stands to sink or bounce. Old Larches bulge with

boles and hold vast Lichen interminglings enmeshed into proximity by an
intimate limited surface, a choice furrow or bark bench. There the Cladonia

clusters intermittent with moss, with grey-green podetia proud like a forest.
Swift Creek braids meltwater-brown below the steep banks of Dogwood

and fills the air with the scurry of matters' aquatic motion. A dark shape
moves in the brown-blue roil and swims upstream. When they reach

the jam of sticks, they porpoise and a club-shaped tail turns last
into the water, a Beaver. Sand Hill Cranes croon rain rattle coiling,

hard to hear above the liquid susurrus. Pipsissewa is still prone, but each
leaf looks eager to tease gravity and gain skyward. Orthilia secunda

summons a wintergreen flavor, but not theirs, one of a Pyrola from afar,
north and east across the continent. It smells like wet Lichen, like tangles

of Bryoria epiphytic on Larch. Usnea draws the air with spores. Time is a
factor of birdsong and precipitation, and the variables are innumerable

and erratic. Hypogymnia's gray thalli grace the forest floor. If I took you
with me, we would both be each of these words and none of them. What is

so, is this spring, and the sprungness pierces us green like Sword Fern and
turns us into a river-scoured pebble, turned over and over like the River in

green sentient minds, chloroplasts gleaning light to part water in order to
free electrons then ferried into everything fraught with life, as in *om*.

Desire
unspools
like
green
globe
chains

of *Anabaena*

a cyanobacteria

prokaryote calls it out

to have a naked nucleus

this gram-negative bacteria

that suffuses rice plants

with essential nitrogen

(fixation of N_2 to NH_3)

all the while finding

while feeding another

they're home

Two Fungal Species Among Many
Play Telephone and Ferret Food

mycorrhizal fungal mycelia
link two or more plants

mediators among trees
they slip sugars and sip whispers

Rhizopogon vesiculosus
and *Rhizopogon vinicolor*

unique soil patterns spread
like roots in the O horizon

their diverse energy source
secure over space and time

they link trees old and young
trees thriving and flailing

mycorrhizal networks integral to
tree survival, to forest resilience

large trees are hubs, old threads
holding and gifting

trees and their fungi
this web of nurture

like a neural net
cradling life with life

Press Down to be Amazed

pine whites spill from ponderosa boughs
tumble across sky sculling air

wings dissolve into the brine blue night
the way dreams unspool into darkness

then vanish like the perfect web wheel
that fractures as you woods walk

a line between two moods lingers
one end still branch-affixed

the other rippling loose with breath
I want to remember you this way

how prisms cast colors
first invisible in featureless space

then refract vibrance onto any form
even those muddled or disarrayed

Asterisks Indicate Significant Differences

parallel lull, peltate initiate, frost forced, red cymes on burst culms, larix color phase green yellow, yellow-green, gold, the old hoard existential spider, hemiparasitic inflorescence tundra swans rippling the reflections, round expansions, existing tension, torsion on tendrils, the rilled ride, inside the cell walls' polysaccharide, osmotic motion, ameboid invocation, planktons' and diatoms' silt pulse electron hush, blueish cosmos, dry clays arboreal forays, sun-suckled sap, flickers' bark tap, roots hoist water, arbuscular tether

Foraging Behavior of the Wood-rotting Fungus

Phanerochaete velutina spiders ki's mycelium
exploratory mode makes whirls
dichotomous branches split
      & split again
            a wheel of touch
            a search of sugar
proliferating pinwheels
pulse radially, extensions of
these fractal dimensions
when the fungus finds food
ki prunes the links
                of lack
o cord-forming basidiomycete
mover of nutrients & carbon, I
      want to know
      how you decide
at the interface of the litter layer
      & soil horizon

I too sieve for insight
      fingers trace hyphae, I
envy cell-level directional memory

because resource depletion
because fractal lack, I

pinwheel & split again

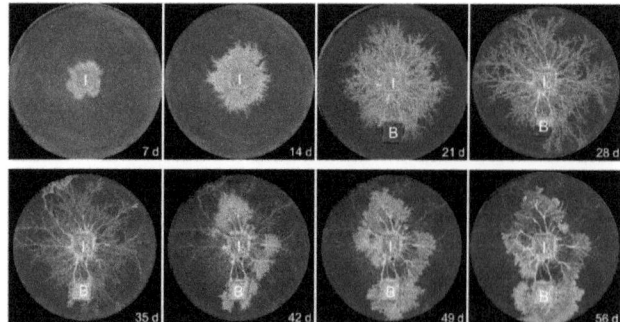

from Fukasawa & Kaga (supplemental material)

BIOLOGY

How We See Photons' Slight Glimmer

1. Refraction of light entering the eye

only in sight
vision sanctuary
nature of materials
and beings is to break
smooth sailing an anomaly
the making and unmaking
reduced dimensionality
shadowy rock stacks
retrace the stone steps
pink, textured, free
the skies of light
she coveted
and covered
with ink

2. Focusing of image on the retina by accommodation of lens

myofibrils muscle fibers
muscle memory
fibers retracting
pulling apart
myoglobin
heme sent
O_2 hungry
subliminal retraction
fibers sliding unhindered, rendered
per your opaque questioning
boundaries not secure
not a stable moment
marbling retreat

3. Convergence of image

turn slightly inward

       see the water

drip

       into the small pools

                lined with pine

                  needles fallen

offer hand   with seed

       entreat the mountain chickadees

                black-capped drops down

       forages   afar

       the dark wet wood is quiet   birds stay silent

brown bark   drips dark   slick with rain

       moss glows sun-green seen

         & water-full

4. Photo-chemical activity in retina and conversion into neural impulse

                  splintering

             impulses seek seenness

             image and consequence

              stimulus and response

               retina 0.5mm thick

                  splintering

             impulses seek seenness

          retina like a three-layer cake

              synaptic connections

           frosting two neural layers

                  splintering

             impulses seek seenness

retina includes
both the sensory neurons
that respond to light
and intricate neural circuits
that perform the first stages
of image processing

hyperpolarized cells
transmit the neural signal

splintering
impulses seek seenness

5. Processing in brain and perception

fen as ark flicker
I saw it redden
how do I get it back
thorn of a thought
extinction burden
if into the junco's trill
fumble of latticed molecules
clickety-clack of what comes

We take the rotary ride

and it squirms around
like a phospholipid bilayer
yet somehow hovers slower
like a studded swell, phosphorus
in my mind's eye orange as agoseris
tawny fiery orange, aura of giant suns
fatty acids undulating, fluid like sea grass
flicked by the tides' pulse, a synaptic zing
we are flung

Evolved to Make Metabolic Sense

lean into the botanical theater
eyeless and mouthless
a single celled remembrance
calls body as host
ATP cleaves and bursts while we dream
see capability as catabolism and anabolism
the extent of perfusion
a billion hungry mitochondria
an interlaced web of want
as such death a false disaster
fertility builds multitudes
delayed resonance
a mere suggestion of self
no fusion of form
just a tangle of genomes
we speak from cells inside cells
this tenuous union

Ensnaring The Pain Burden

whooshing over plain human misery
the day's rhythm-hymn
spangled veil of a dull pull

reverberating across earth's electric ear
loss-howls, breakages, degradation
advanced degeneration

and the quotidian pain
chronic pain
pain ensnaring
the mind struck agony-stung

pathologic entity
pain burden that drags down
pain as a disease
enormous global burden

pain as a definite pathologic state
pain as precious and meaningful tool
pain as psychical adjunct of an imperative, protective reflex
       neurophysiological aspects

pain as inaudible howl
a tearing
keening for cessation

in its late phases, when it becomes intractable, it no longer serves a useful purpose and then
becomes, through its mental and physical effects, a destructive force

harsh discord dictates days
fixed ache grating
sharp pull of disintegration

chronic pain
pain which persists past the normal time of healing
spangled veil of a dull pull

pain starts like a cloud seed
devours everything
persists like a scaffold
coaxes thoughts to a dark tangle

disease *an impairment of the normal state of the living animal or plant body or one of its parts that interrupts or modifies the performance of the vital functions*

pain as a tearing
inaudible howl
keening for cessation

Three main aspects characterizing a disease are 1) the presence of an impairment of the normal functions, 2) the presence of a specific symptomatology, and 3) a distinct etiopathogenesis.

etiopathogenesis *the cause and development of a disease or abnormal condition*

chronic pain as disease
as disabling condition
as intractable destructive force
as grimace, contort, clench, flinch

incessant remorseless neurons know no sleep
          synapses keep firing
blood pools
     in cerebral areas aroused by pain

     synapses keep firing
               fixed attention
inaudible howl

chronic pain affects every aspect of a patient's life, contributing to a loss of both physical and emotional function, affecting a patient's levels of activity (ability to work at home and job and engage in social and recreational pursuits)

sweep of attention
pendulum of a metronome
spangled veil of a dull pull
severe chronic pain
increased death risk
sweep of attention

pendulum of a metronome

wholly independent of the motion
seldom a time when the feeling fades
chronic pain loses its biologic damage signaling function
devastating psychophysiologic consequences

focus on the sound of breath
focus on the sound of breathing

chronic pain neural mechanisms gone awry
maldynia *bad pain*

eudyinia *good pain*
a symptom of an underlying pathological disorder, either an illness or an injury
maldynia *bad pain*
pathological pain, referring to pain as a neuropathological disorder or disease process that occurs due to changes at cellular and molecular levels

bad pain, pain as failure, pain as jailer, as jagged gate

persistent pain
pathologic reorganization of the neural system
wasn't always this way, used to be able to
don't want to feel this
step into the absence, swallow this dullness

point to where it hurts
nocireceptor
          sensory receptor for painful stimuli
where does it hurt

pain urges people to interrupt ongoing activity, elicits protective responses that paradoxically increase interference with daily activities, and compromises the sense of self

how are you today
fine, how are you

grimace, contort, clench, flinch
pain reduces cognitive ability
steals attention
grimace, contort, clench, flinch

imaging studies have revealed that information about tissue damage is distributed at
multiple forebrain sites involved in attentional, motivational, and cognitive aspects of the
pain experience

attention is a mechanism of selection of information
to protect the coherence of action
attention is a selection mechanism for action
select actions steal attention

mutatis mutandi the necessary changes
other things being equal
pain is designed to interrupt
does not easily relinquish this capacity
pain as failure, pain as jailer, as jagged gate

sweep of attention
pendulum of a metronome
spangled veil of a dull pull
strive to bring the interruptive effects
          of pain back to its basics
where is the pain today
grimace, contort, clench, flinch

the perceived intensity of unilateral pain evoked by different inputs correlates with increases
in regional cerebral blood flow in primarily five structures: bilaterally in the thalamus, the
contralateral insula, the bilateral premotor cortex, the contralateral anterior cingulate, and
the cerebellar vermis

wholly independent of the motion
seldom a time when the feeling fades

attentional bias in the development and maintenance of chronic pain
optimism a resilience factor
sleep a silken banner of roseate respite

pain is a complex and subjective conscious experience constructed and modulated by a
constellation of sensory, cognitive, and affective factors

increased attention on the location
oscillations of iterative torque and tension
numerical scale of agony

meditation may reduce pain by fine-tuning the amplification of nociceptive sensory events
through top-down control processes

increase attention on the sensation of breath

the cognitive state of mindfulness meditation–based analgesia does not reduce pain through
one avenue but rather multiple, unique neural mechanisms

grimace, contort, clench, flinch

dissolve the spangled veil of the dull pull
diffuse attention away
from the inaudible howl
from the harsh discord that dictates days
from the fixed ache grating
from the sharp pull of disintegration

let go of arising sensory events
of grimace, contort, clench, flinch
without judgment
perceived sensory and affective events
are momentary and fleeting
do not require further evaluation

pain as quantifiable, reduceable, and past
pain eliminable
wholly independent of the motion

dissolving the veil

$f(p) = \mid t - (b)^{(n-1)} \mid$

$f(\text{pain}) = \mid \text{time} - (\text{increased attention on the sensation of breath})^{(\text{iterations-1})} \mid$

pain as function of
focusing on the sensation of breath
focusing on the sensation of grimace, contort, clench, flinch
focus on the sensation of breath
focusing on the sharp pull of disintegration

focus on the sensation of breathing

focusing on the inaudible howl

focus on the sensation of breath

focus on the sensation of breathing

focus on the sensation of breath

To travel arteriorly

like a bolus pulse

    external atom flex

valence level up

    to slip laterally

like iron in heme

    a visceral listen

fat like a clot

Mother of Pearl, or One of the Manifestations

growth
and self-assembly
nacreous lacquer
snail miracle
mother of pearl

grown by
successive nucleation
of aragonite crystals
and their arrest

manifestations
of self-organization
self-assembly

the holes in their shells
were for breathing

mechanism of c-axis aragonite growth arrest
by the deposition of a protein layer

thickness of the aragonite platelets
      a constant (0.5 μm)

the holes in the shells
were for breath

      powerful   crack   deflectors
           viscoplastic   deformation
     tensile   strength   bricklike
Self-assembly is one of the manifestations of self-organization.

The holes in the shells were for breathing.

orthorhombic crystals
     often twinned
     and pseudo-hexagonal
              in cross-section

the two forms of $CaCO_3$, calcite   *rhombohedral*

and aragonite   *orthorhombic*
constitute the inorganic component
          this ceramic/organic composite
          95 wt.% ceramic, 5 wt.% organic material

the external layer   *prismatic calcite*
the internal region   *aragonite*

abalone's mantle epithelium secretes chemicals that produce growth
          ejects them into   extrapallial   space

biomineralization

small, terraced cones
on the growth surface
little trees

self-assembly
          is one of the manifestations
                    of self-organization
the holes
          in the shells   were for breathing

calcium ions on the face; carbon, oxygen

growth bands
          mesolayers

(a) Random nucleation of aragonite crystals on protein.

                    no beginning of emote, mote of atoms
                         assembly a swell of telos
                    as krills' choreographed swirl
               a trill of time, matter directional
                    held fast from a center
                         centrifugal flare
                    a snare of minerals
               scaffolded on amino acids
                    placid iridescence
                    such smoothness

(b) Lateral growth in (a, b) directions.

not content to be unilateral
planar, or flat, but full in expansion
ordered and expansive, regular
in growth, earnest structure
manifest of Mollusca
iridescent dance
temporal range
cretaceous to present
Haliotis
abalone

(c) Second growth spurt after deposition of beta sheet and
       nucleation.

mother-of-pearl

mother

mother *of*

pearl mother

(d) First aragonite plates are butted together while
growth of second layer continues in a and b directions.

what makes rainbows
the sheen of vision
green flash over the sea at sunset
waves engulfed by the sunset swale
shimmers pink and turquoise green
trees hefting their hue
smoothness its resilience
brittle platelets and elastic biopolymers
stacked into brickwork
this color whorl
welded whole

(e) Nucleation of third layer as second layer growth
continues in a and b directions.

                              corollary
                               corolla
                                aura
                             color coil
                              abalone
                         mother of pearl

mixture of brittle platelets and the thin layers of elastic
biopolymers makes the material strong and resilient
self-assembly is one of the manifestations of self-
organization the holes in the shells were for breathing

ORNITHOLOGY

Brindle
Brown

remembering
is not seeing

transformation

cliff to rocks

these avian ascents

next comes pillars
of clotted coal

his sinister humors

ibis cloaked with soot

insatiable
bellow

now rises the raven

black clear
against sulfur skies

where a paler bird

would be

lost

When Birds Drink Seawater Salt Moves Through Their Blood Into Salt Glands And Out Of Their Bodies

after H.D.

lift my head—help me up—there—
do I not deserve to drink deep of the mineral wet—

take me to the mountains—o for wings to seek
the purple marsh—sky-space—honey-fragrant
—bliss-source inviolable—the rock-shelf rookery
osprey preying over the salt-beach—salt-air sand-stuck—

lift my head—help me up—there—where water becomes
brackish—then all salt recedes—I can taste the glacial till
ultramarine-green mineral grains ground to flour—

help me there—lift my sky-space into the purple marsh
praying to the mineral mountains—for wings to speak—

White Horizon
Over
Black-Green Woods

North Fork
      silent mornings
      and a flushed
      grouse

Bryoria lichen
      tinseled
      by rime

rainbow argillite
      river-scoured
      till-sculpted

November
      ice feeds
      on itself

open water
      shrinks
      into a
      small
      pool

few mallards
      and swans
      linger

now
      diminishing
      waters

birds
      cold cast
      ice exiled

      gone

A Museum of Bohemian Waxwings, March 5th

the flock centers its irruptive orbits
around the cherry and cottonwood trees

an expansive twitter and chatter
fills the snow-grey sky

my gaze of intention settles on
yellow-tipped tails, defiant head-crests

branches quiver and still
each motion creates a wing flurry

they say joy must be self-taught
again and again, continuous

see grief as a knot unraveling
with their every movement

the centrality of their sound-smear
the wringing out of expectation

out from the branches they rise and feed
find fruits from a more vibrant season

return to the cottonwood
seek the swell of red sap stirring

still gleaning, still searching
find sweetness in what remains

Go Away, It's Spring

rosettes green, ferns leaf forth
conjuring wild flourish
among them lurk lacerations—
think I'd let them follow me?

water under all, crystalline need
aquatic taint cloying
magnetic hollow culm—
don't let the poison in

jay in the lodgepole
fractal branches and whorled cones
invisible, blue honed plumage
homage to the new ones
the avian arrivals, kinglets and swallows—
don't sacrifice this bliss

linger under spring
advance the leaves
the insects, this alliance
of vibratory verdure
every vibrance—
think thinking endures?

You Can Tell It's a Mountain Chickadee
By The White Stripe Above the Eye

These obscure calyces
boast saturated hues

dawn winds swirl
arc tendrils supine

epiphytic lichens spin
wreath the greatest branches

glib spring spreads lupine wings
blue-purple banners and keels

sap-sweet vanilla air
eddies out over meadowrue

the swell of May bursts
sun rises over marsh sedges

if winter taught me anything
it was carved by cold and scour

by land hued like mountain chickadee eggs
flat white, sometimes red-speckled

now their sweet whistles thread the glade
I shadow and sit below in the snowberry

find the unfurled flower
tease apart foliate fronds

I hear how calendula petals

taste on my tongue
orange hungry ascent
bee dance in the wood's rose
pollen plucking hum
loud floral whirl
whole note yellow swale
glass-clear peal of posy
nighthawk's uncanny twang
midnight's minor chords
wingbeat hootenanny
bittern sound bite, ear cheer
vitreous susurrus
fox sparrow belting it out
fir and marsh marigold lyrics
ossicles' audible auras
acapella katydid choir
hot click of cricket hops
full trill chord of summer
ethereal material soundstream
flicker's beak-plucked hymn
that song again

BOTANY

Merry Quotidian

in the tensile
slant of errant silence—

ask as though seen
sing as though cast

into devil's club
Oplopanax horridus

thorn stung, a terror mirror
or savior, all similar horrors

in the chaos, as though stillness
was devil, spined, with blood-red berries

palmate leaves that dwarf our palms
we the creator and destroyer of worlds

also created and destroyed
as matter coils and recoils

is absorbed and adorned—
sing as though spun

listen as though gutted
nail snared, ether aired

among the moans
sing the stung, even as

electrons spin symmetric—
merry spark slake, merry slick slip

conjure excitatory gestures
generous myelin meanders

merry mineral and visceral
cross that snow snare

angular as though Araliaceae
crystal as though cast

Arise All Tendrils

emptied of breath the night wind waits
drenched branches bow to the garden

iron slips deep beneath dank desire
you intuit what twines within it

rain splits shadows into syllables
darkness drapes cotyledons

elements stir in the nocturnal soil
fragments of nutrients find form

tonight in the first spring flutter
you dress yourself with lichens

you lean in to lick the shoots
green is the heard hallelujah

when stars spill indigo ethereal
the electron essence empties itself

you rise to cultivate these green galaxies
like rootlets sprung from a stellate maze

Tatters tore
at the people

yet their dreams

were beautiful

like the alders at first spring

unseen intricacies synching

chlorophyll sneaking up synapses

catkins and leaf buds

deity-green

Is it a Plant Feedback Loop

that sends me downstairs
to hold the *Book of Leaves*

to flip through stiff pages
recall green contents

I find myself opening
to the rubber tree page

Ficus elastica

rubber fig, rubber bush
India rubber tree

whose natural rubber source
fell out of importance
since synthetic inventions

yet was first inferiorized by
the unrelated rubber tree
Hevea brasiliensis

this book of leaves asserts
I may make a skeleton
out of rubber tree leaves

remnants
of wax shined leaves
would loom
like a milk lattice
of ghost veins

I think of my
Ficus elastica
upstairs

survivor of harsh
indoor conditions

when blooming
it's pollinated
by fig wasps

o my waist-high tree
you are never
to flower here

yet now I remember
it's time to give you some water

Potential Additional Research

aggregated seed and moss pods
Syntrichia moss
            twisted star moss
            whose leaves wick fog
            conspicuously squarrose-recurved
            & furl to brown when dry (poikilohydry)

if spatial or temporal distribution matters
to moss, to lichen, to science, to us

then is it the same brown-eyed sunshine lichen
         (*Vulpicida canadensis*)

if I am still behind glass
as when I am touching it?

skin touches hyphae
fluorescent from vulpinic acid

         some interest
         good candidates

leave the door open

we support the idea

Consider the Plant's Perspective

bur-clover burr   right
run   toward the center
where the cotyledons
rise   against thirteen
tongue-like barriers

our roots hoist water
up   through the xylem column
surge to the topmost of branches

botanically simple plants
spored   and old
we complete the cycle

samaras carry seeds at our heart
as far as the wing   will take us
pirouetting with life's promise

once awakened   we grow quickly
radicle gravity coaxed
plumule crests   coil and flare
above the A horizon

silvery rime catches us watching

a tribe of trees contains we

Why Not Inhabit Sunlight?

not yet ferned, deeplier
flanked with devil's club—

paint us back our picture
before fracture, verdant rupture

brush strokes center color
time bends
back to brilliance

crimson paintbrush
& later perideridia
an Apiaceae whorl

greenness
as percussive lull

inflorescence allures even as
thoughts trawl the blue-dark contours
        of the seafloor, moor there—

why not inhabit sunlight—
        where branches
        bifurcate, radiate
        & ferns reign
        over felsic intrusions
        flawless, never otherwise

photosynthetic fugue stirs
the green gust, circuitous—

why not inhabit sunlight?

        not yet ferned, deeplier, where
        juncos coax time lucid
        & ethereal theories
        rest wrought,
        hungry, ungulate—

consciousness persists
in moss-dressed gneiss

Study of Achenes

take calendula's achenes
or agoseris' sculpt-sway

grown in the microbial parade
dirt dropped & genome scripted

take monstered chains
achenes of answering

anthro-throttled
overcome/succumbed

plumbed extinct
distinct death ensconced

post-Eocene
snared with sound

this rasp of milkweed
that wed achenes with wind

before the dim damage
acuminate sepals

this geranium sunshine
green whorls swirl palmate

prism-tethered
pleat of the inevitable

plucked from our acid ocean
what plaits my consciousness

this quiver synapse
a lapse in hybridity

liquid and yoked
the bees are at the nepeta

when will the colibri come
achenes dry, indehiscent, one seeded

from which we arise
the chromatic nixes monochrome

thoughts wind-dispersed
anemochory

ven diagram of infinity
we are a spur of maya

excised only in mind
contracting and spiraled

like the maples' winged
achenes, samaras

enveloped in it
when we arc into pose

arms atmosphere up
myofibrils slip wide

do you see the sky swirls
mimicking you in cloud-speak

fever-mirror encircles
this inevitable geranium sunset

plucked into particulates
finite mica flick

ASTRONOMY & ATMOSPHERIC SCIENCE

Ramping Up

Rearing up like a cicada storm
        the sun is accelerating its tantrums

after seven years of relative calm
        the sun will be more temperamental

light slips under the canopy and plaits the forest floor
        there's fire enough between the voids—

heat rushes up toward the threshold
        this solar scream to echo earth's howl

sun ticks out an eleven-year cycle
        oscillates between quiescent and hyperactive

solar paroxysm breaches false stasis
        solar scream falls deaf on our ears

knocks satellites into the atmosphere's edge
        to be gobbled up by fire

there's fire enough between the voids—

today no sun to be seen
        snow-obscured mountains
mere apparition

subliminal in the singe of storm
        violent eruption
coronal mass ejection

kinetic energy addition
        snow sliding
unhindered

sun gifts particles to our atmosphere
        extreme ultraviolet

reminds us of our incandescent center
        can we make room for more mass

how do we account
        for these gifts

the sun's diaphanous upper atmosphere
        corona asymmetric
full halo

one million degrees blistering
          things sparkle in it

matter differentially intimate
                    sun catalyzes
the dissolute

sloughs fire into our upper air
          spits into space
incoherent essence

clouds fracture to parade the sun
          for now pale and sallow
for now hovering insect-like

no static solar face
          no stasis
there's fire enough between the voids—

so much gnashing
          can we weather
this waxing and waning

blood-red slippage
          or fluidity of matter

Altocumulus lenticularis

Lenticular clouds cloak
constant movement
look static, yet ferocious
layers of whipped vapor
frayed by wind's teeth
white tatters
and layers of water
orographic wave clouds
lens-shaped, draped
like time's sediment
striated like the canyon's
belly, iron-stained and mafic
lenticular, ice-pressed cirrus slant
curvature various, vicious to avians
and aviation, air elation, oxygen
generation gusts, hydrophilic, aqueous
questions, ions, caught in the fervent torrent
atmospheric current, swept over cloaked peaks
forming and dissipating, eternal death-birth
splayed loop layered over water, skyward

Grief, unlike stars

wavers   more   when distant

      a constancy
               dense atomic   flow

   clutches   close grief
          leaden core   stars have a better chance

of   quivering   when   close
         atmospheric   sleight of hand

light   bent
                 and   distorted
varying   temperatures \ densities of air

      if there is
          no twinkle
    if there is
            no grief

      atmospheric   scintillation

    convection currents   coax
         loss   of seeing conditions
     incoming cold fronts   replace warmer
               air

'bad seeing'   astronomers complain

'good seeing' troposphere quelled calm

   now good seeing   sets light straight

     close loss   has a better chance   of salt

  as time \ distance increases

     tears   become notable

   had a cry   cold front moves in

auras shudder
      give off erratic light   mere mirages

        tomorrow practice   *good seeing*
good compassion
     the atmosphere   stills
   reveals
    no close   grief
    no twinkle

Cold mountain feeling

the rime crystals
       scoured out on cornices
lenticulars over St. Mary
       the crowned jewel
       of winter's raw splendor
       grief-rendered
black-blue refraction of sunlit reds
       inked black
two treecreepers—always skyward—
       they find the pine's furrows
       tailfeathers brace bark
wind crackles ice-laced quince
       long days of shadow
       & rainbow peaks

Completely Blocked by the Occluding Body

thin-edged moon
      slopes into infinity
correlation   of whispering cosmos
    to ice   this axial tilt   obliquity
 reflection of constellations
      no fixed consciousness
residuum of umbra
            embrace of buoyancy
all right action   leads to oracular   oration
     one concave enclave   save
        revelation   elocution
born on the ecliptic plane   tallying   revolutions
        no common   longevity
no lunar fixity
      silver sliver never final   while
   failing light's   full hail   falls

Space Just Landed

no one calls meteors

        celestial spit

yet that doesn't stop

     them from

         plummeting—

sprung   hurled

as through

    a breached   cell   wall

exudate and delivered

       mineral-laden

arriving in a void mood

a blip   from a hole without   color

lured out

       as exit
as interface

one iota

   of the cosmic furl

just one

   pearly-whirled

       facet

GEOLOGY

Please Provide Proof of Universal Schism

For instance, here exists this
usnea lichen that haloes a pyramid
like a cosmic coil, elemental eye ablaze.
One point a compression of simultaneity
of fixity and its form is found only here
in my home, where my body only
approximates bilateral symmetry, or minerality.
Its base is agate, striated ochre and sienna
a regular square pyramid, this lithic flamelet
and here twines the sacred spiral
of fungi and algae, pocketed from the forest
around the time of solstice, fingered for its filaments
its dichotomous drape, flattened and open to light
poised over this lithic abyss, luminous.

Gneiss of the Cascades Core
or O Orogenesis

mountain pose
body still over rock

these folded and heated upheavals
            some of which
are concordant

our own orogenesis
            preferred orientation
of platy minerals

finite fixed forms
            flung upon
elongate grains
            and grain aggregates

these non-coaxial
            deformational features

this composite fabric
            faulted and folded
45 years is not 4540 million

yet minerals slip my skin
            proteins misfold and falter

the deep crustal evolution
            of magmatic arc
is enigmatic

to elucidate the origin:
            textural analysis, bulk rock chemistry,
            mineral chemistry, thermodynamic modeling

this lineation
            defined
by mineral alignment
            mica, garnet, and tourmaline

our lineation
            defined by lack

angle into triangle pose
            arms parallel to peaks

this foliation is born from
        micas, compositional layering
and elongation of
        quartz and plagioclase

most common mineral order (paragenesis):
        garnet + kyanite + quartz +
        plagioclase + biotite + muscovite

we build our own only mineral
        inorganic, crystalline, solid
our rocks, our bones

hydroxyapatite
        calcium phosphate mineral
$Ca_5(PO_4)_3(OH)$

O orogenesis
O innumerable linkages

        coherent crystallites
whose patterns identify
        and name
           and also by fracture

born from geological processes

earthen cauldrons
        stir silica tetrahedrons
            SiO_4^{4-}
silicate minerals
        build mountains

lithic iterations
           identical atom clusters
        color spun

malachite
        named for mallow leaves
$Cu_2CO_3(OH)_2$
        copper carbonate hydroxide mineral

green banded
        each band
        marks
        growth episodes

absorbed
        and reprecipitated

o fixed lattice
        embedded in us

we gather these
        minerals
this earth
this life

bodies fold and rise
        born and built betwixt
life a mineral matrix

and
        it goes
on from
        there
in definite
        crystalline
structures

Quartz Cliffs Not Broken by Rime

each face mirrors the spark-sheen
      and the liquid torque
      of ultramarine lashes

do the seas favor you?

obsidian flakes
      splinter into sand

waves arc wild
      over angular basalt

do the seas favor you?

if I whisk the salt spray
      from purpled plagioclase

if a sinuous slip of light
      breaches blue shadow

would your flawless face
      refract the facets?

PHYSICS & MATH

Nor Could the Sun

after Archibald MacLeish "Einstein"

       — tones equidistant, fervent
        sweet music make

but it seems assured
she ends
her hands,   which are decorticate
      disintegrate
          for suddenly she feels—
a sleep-wake drift spate
    cognate
whence   she knows
each calyx
      undifferentiated
            outstretched on the earth
she puts out leaves
      and although they seize
           integrated electron furls
—but the sepals
     [vitreous chimes]

    when in a moment she occupies—
—but the sepals
          petals   fugue-fused—
now no   words
    [overflow]

she lies upon her bed
         atomic
she can count the first
  sharp glimmer
if they will not speak—
        basalt torrents rapt
        on iron rails
whence begins
             each plummety paradox
still she stands—
       careful to follow
           each aural centrifuge
           each utterance
for which she shall feel,   infuse
this element
       [however fire-fraught]
like a body
which seems to keep—

Show
How It Might
Be So

If DNA holds light fast and
if unraveled symmetry rivals validity
then water remembers more
than just the shape of matter

If the body's photons excite a full spectrum of frequencies
if each cell has its own unique set it's sending forth
then two molecules can resonate together, can resonate more
than those molecules that are spinning apart

If DNA holds light fast and
if symmetry varies with density
then water remembers more
than just the shape of matter

If both specific molecules and intermolecular bonds emit certain
specific frequencies that can be detected billions of light-years away
if electronic frequencies are accepted to preside in the living
then living matter
can be moved to accept sound as proxy, becomes
like water unable forget the sounds of structures
cohered into seeking
source-shape effects

If DNA holds light fast and
if photons are massless
then water remembers more

sound shapes the meaning of matter
light catches the meaning
and weaves it through water
superradiance
discordant energy organizes
into coherent photons

If light and DNA hold fast
if validity unravels matter
more than water remembers
then vibrations rival shapes

If tensile subatomic talk and
if exquisite coherences are result rhythms
then this shows how it's more
than just the light
it's the show

The heart refuses circumference

a regular dodecahedron appears twice—

      convex Platonic solid looms angular

stellations of the convex form
          from which every dreary vacuity vacates

      rescinds its n-honeycomb

tessellation in any number of dimensions

      space filling   and combinatorial
                the shape
                looms
        over the sea
      in an enigmatic Dali illustration
    like an apparition

            whorl of five faces
            twelve-sided polyhedral
regular star dodecahedra
      when freed from perfection
    you are pyrite —

and we
flitting fast
    inside the mass
        of twelve faces
      as if
our hearts
    inhabited   ordinary Euclidian space

a moveable
    swell   beating against flatness
        refusing regularity   or
angularity
      embroidering   constellations

echoing quartz's
    piezoelectricity
        fast upon these rocks
    cosmos's
ferrous throes

Be Still, Mere Molecule

The obvious storms coax secondary revery
        frigid enkindling
fitful forests
        trumpet radial shadows

then at long last the ice recedes
        and the first bird-wakes ripple the open water
now receding from the clutch
        of winter's first currency, cold

cold that held the air sub-silent
        against the mountain chickadees' chatter
and now in their dapple chat
        we hear the ascension of spring

warm-aspect shrubs appear empowered
        grass-thin leaves venture out

cold night cuts away the artifice
        residuum of persistence, this ice
        that regrows as matter slows
hydrogen atoms bind into a hexagon
        space increases
        and density decreases

ice crusts the liquid
        loosely bonded and spaceless
waters are ablaze with a cottonwood wind
        be still, mere molecule, mere matter
be still despite whirring valences

buds thrash against cerulean streaks
        the equinox picks apart stuck snow
finds the ground tilt-warmed
        waiting for the thaw

There Will Be Harmonies

cumulative values
what is the foundation
anodic (forward) and cathodic (reverse) reactions
scarlet bluffs and sage
harvest of thought
of what significance
entire system of shrilling shadow
frankly, charm and brightness
trout symphonies and wet stones
quick to plunge into glossy undulations
concentric currents
viscosity and liquid ululations
universal common intercept

The reaction rate theory for viscosity is a statistical mechanical theory
that assumes a liquid has a quasi-crystalline structure and consists of
molecules vibrating about an equilibrium position.

Under the reaction rate theory framework, a molecule can only move
when:

1) there is an empty hole available to jump in

and 2) the molecule has sufficient energy to overcome the attractive
forces exerted by surrounding molecules.

The energy necessary to form a hole with the size of a molecule in the
liquid is assumed to be the same as that to vaporize a molecule.

: the most irrational liquid number
: constant intertwining of light and loss
: volume of dream cones
: ultramarine ideal constant
: temperature of waxing grief

Based on the reaction rate theory, the free activation energy of viscous
flow is linked to the liquid viscosity through the following expression:

$$\eta = \frac{Nh}{V}\exp\left(\frac{\Delta E_a}{RT}\right)$$

where:

    N: the Avogadro's number

    h: Plank's constant

    V: <u>molar volume</u>

    R: ideal gas constant

    T: temperature

nothing illusory
broadening and gradually slackening
returning to glass stillness, viscous surface
stained by polychrome hues
intermittently mottled, darker, narrower
there will be harmonies
frankly, charm and brightness
quick to plunge into shrilling shadow

If We Change the Same Set of Basic Physics Equations

those that determine velocity and resistance

from water to air to outside the atmosphere

where one small push, really a   nudge

can send one into a   radical   trajectory

radical for speed   and for   lack of resistance
where speed holds   and matter wheels by

then we would have a different
equation   for elation

also a function
of the intricate present

this conifer forest   fraught

with ice and stillness   spruce burst of
old girth, spruce-lemon

needle crush   a hush of crossbills
and after their twitter follows

I throw shadows   through

the spruce-fir forest   my

descent like a plummet— yet   flying

elated, firs
needling the
fog down below

water crystals a cradle
a glint of frost
descent of sharp joy
buoyant
above
the din

CHEMISTRY

Wood Parade

Pour, pour down matter   like lava flowing into rock

pour through   like air whisked through slot canyons

       carved sandstone   snaking   below   rivers of sky

    striated   like waves on silt

        cobalt light lashes over wood grains

layers notch time with lignin

          each year rung like a badge

light   expanse following   a dark stop

          now atoms rearrange

            bonds heat-singed

     pyrolysis

         atoms and energy   release

unbound atoms   now hot blue   mingle with ambient O_2

     glowing gas   not the former tree   spooky blue

      vibrations become heat

    a fire whorl

          orange

       dervish

      flickering   with life-pulse

   cindered

     & smoke licked

        these breakages

years   unraveling into ash

       &

        a red rift

Marginalia on The Table of Elements
Including Names, Symbols, and Atomic Numbers

H Hydrogen (1) Hydrogen the original engine, electrons spinning, sparse valence.

He Helium (2) Helium the heliotrope, an isotope, spacious sparseness.

Li Lithium (3) Lithium the thirsty one, a thrum of three, plucked from infinite.

Be Beryllium (4) Beryllium the better gem, better blue-green hue, 4-merous, beryl.

B Boron (5) Boron like Boötes fixed like a flared flicker, rooted, marooned.

C Carbon (6) Carbon cut to curtsy and clutch, a fan of life's geometry, its pillars.

N Nitrogen (7) Nitrogen near nuisance, or sustenance, cycling sky and sea.

O Oxygen (8) Oxygen of generative breath, of wind's immersive simmer.

F Fluorine (9) Fluorine the fixed ef, effulgent if fluorite, then as flux to foster fluidity.

Ne Neon (10) Neon the inert one, concentrated in the cosmos, noble one, near none.

Na Sodium (11) Sodium the start of saline, the slake of ask, salt-licked and slack.

Mg Magnesium (12) Magnesium the gamely one, mage, folding like mossy gneiss, mass.

Al Aluminum (13) Aluminum mines mock martyred trees, are blue with blood and bled metal.

Si Silicon (14) Silicon covets sand, sends grains to glass, fastens stones to structure.

P Phosphorus (15) Phosphorus fickle chorus, food for ferns, earned euphoria, florid.

S Sulfur (16) Sulfur the furious, spurious foul, yellow solid, crystalline, hell-fire fuel.

Cl Chlorine (17) Chlorine the original rind, caustic grindstone, dissolving death's DNA.

Ar Argon (18) Argon arguably gone, garish gas, inert newt, from *argos*, idle.

K Potassium (19) Potassium as prelude, precursor, crude crust, predictor of lassitude.

Ca Calcium (20) Calcium scaffold, sealed and seamed, sashed ash, osteoblast.

Cr Chromium (24) Chromium the colored one, steely-grey and lustrous, metallurgic.

Mn Manganese (25) Manganese angling for gain, signaling for manna, mouthing *om*.

Fe Iron (26) Iron round in remorse and railing, or rather square as ether bringer.

Co Cobalt (27) Cobalt the heavy colt, built into blood balm, vitamin B_{12}, myelin.

Ni Nickel (28)   Nickel the naughty sick, the poisoning lick, the stricken fickle, flaxen sack.

Cu Copper (29)   Copper open to carry, like our hemoglobin, hauling O_2 in hemocyanin.

Zn Zinc (30)   Zinc the succulent one, neither zenith nor azure of zinnias, haze blue.

Se Selenium (34)   Selenium into chiral hexagonal crystals, chirality an asymmetry, mirror.

Br Bromine (35)   Bromine brown, born being diatomic molecules in all aggregation states.

Kr Krypton (36)   Krypton rips kites, tinkers with crypt kits, tapers prior pyres, clips.

Rb Rubidium (37)   Rubidium rhubarb darling, bright bits of ruby bitters, bride brims gems.

Sr Strontium (38)   Strontium strum stung, time tainted and strung, staunch stem, mount rant.

Ag Silver (47)   Silver slithers, vilifies flight; reveres virility, verdurous shivers, and rivers.

Cd Cadmium (48)   Cadmium cowers afore dim diamonds, spouts mad claims of maimed clay.

I Iodine (53)   Iodine inks water with interruption, heaviest of the stable halogens, violet.

Xe Xenon (54)   Xenon acts as spheres, strange, foreign, feigned fortress of rareness, zeroed.

Ba Barium (56)   Barium as pyrotechnic pucker, irradiative bare, barite, bright maybe, bar.

Au Gold (79)   Gold the gaudy one, the greedy hold, hot yellow spit, the hallowed grit.

Hg Mercury (80)   Mercury the curious fury, maiden mayhem, merry care, the mad cure.

Pb Lead (82)   Lead us into metallurgic temptation; elemental shepherds, spin our spreads.

> **It would be**
> **just   like   you,**
> **universe,**   to morph the molecular structure of chlorophyll into a flower.

Molecular structure of chlorophyll *a*.

84

Ki is a smoke wisp & I

watch ki twist in the wind. Energy bifurcates, unfurls into long lines of grey, twines from the incense stick at the seam between what is formed & what fire turns to ash. Ki moves like a rivulet from a moss trickle, wavelets beside ki, dance of intense dissolution & the farther ki spirals from the seam, ki becomes undiscernible, dissolute, scatters into invisible fractals, sparse likeness of original form, verdant garden to ghost, holding no fidelity to coherent essence, until sparseness of space ungrasps cohere, all form flared and fled, no near body, no more ki to see.

And In This Regard We Breathe Shapes

deciduous or coniferous, all trees fill the air with theirs

give off compounds to speak, protect, warn, repel, or proclaim
forest trees exude terpenes and terpenoids

      biogenic volatile organic compounds (BVOCs)

each plant species emits a mixture of up to 200 different compounds

terpenes and terpenoids ameliorate inflammation
      by inhibiting inflammatory processes
      forest-bathing, woods-breathing, healing

23 common forest BVOC's

    α-Pinene Camphene α-Phellandrene Terpinolene
1,8-Cineole (Eucalyptol)   Terpinen-4-ol Bornyl acetate
   Humulene (α-Caryophyllene)   β-Pinene   Myrcene
   β-Phellandrene Camphor Linalool d-Limonene
   β-Caryophyllene (trans-Caryophyllene)   3-Carene
      α-Terpinene   p-Cymene   Linalool-oxide
      γ-Terpinene Sabinene α-Terpineol Borneol

and in this regard we breathe shapes

uncertain bells with the teeth of water
that may be seen to guard oblivion

illustrated by the in-depth studies
of the hazardous abyss
and of the second ring closure
of terrestrial dust and floral fire

final proton abstraction yields the final product

mawkish meridians and garish compounds

although investigated extensively
        using sophisticated approaches

things still fall apart

greater conformational constraints
the data do not betray us

regardless of the catalytic cascade
forests have been deemed therapeutic

these notions have been experimentally tested
because of the multitude of reaction products

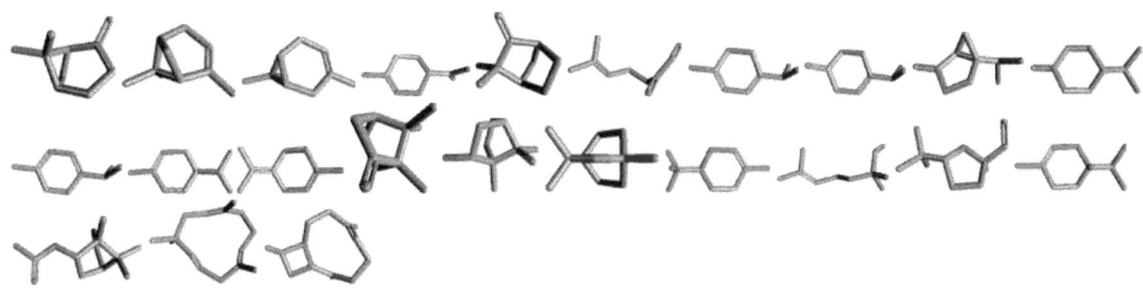

ENVIRONMENTAL SCIENCE

I dream we are Anthropocene torture machines

and every time we use a resource
like gas for hot water to wash hands
something on the other end must die
for every gift a tally on content, and corpses—
energetically earnestly intent and coiled tight
yet the golden-crowned kinglet collides with glass
lies still with feathers vibrant still
a shock of yellow straight-streaked and cold
a few feet from the song sparrow
who lives in the shrubby cinquefoil, emerging
as if from a beaver's den, taking breaks to swim air
for fodder, then plucking back to inner depths
brown-striated body plumbing sugar from fallen plants
flitting in between dichotomous branches—
o life, o convoluted shadows of shelter, our altars
bundles of energy spinning, spun out & sprung
like vertiginous vert to senescence
all the while valences' still plump with electrons
spinning hither without falter

Heavy Metal Hangover

mercury fixed   we are

        swept sick

from   chemical drift

    flung from

a dolt's dither
        a slurry of slick

plucked from Prop 65's lists

toxic valences cleave
    base   pairs

a riotous rupture

a nauseous crush

methylmercury
    and its
      compounds

DNA death-nuisance

mutagenic monster—answer

    was it you?

Ashes Again

fouled tranquils

hard-planed planks
  coated by scarlet scars

  remove each clarity?
      summon
        scope
sufficient   to see them?

consider a lack of raindrops
        bees again

  pervasive air quality alert, likewise
nonsensical algorithms
                        and oblivions

comets eating their own tails

  chemicals murmuring
  over pivotal orbits

attune to
        the blue-green gesture
        or crepuscular
            cirrus stutter

evasive and common

        like contracting
        fibrinogen
or
        a slither-clade

        to which
    we shall
        clasp

Keep Your Hands Inside
the Anthropocene at All Times

We feel toxins fix in us—
wash [hydraulic fracking fluid]
from our wounds

We open out   to light
recoil when we
reach oil—
        rootlets shudder

We feel malignancy
                course in us
death script rewritten—
        pulse of ceaseless growth

We seek
        the sapphire cloud mirror
plummet into leachate—
        asphyxiate

We hear a grotesque roar-machine
a quickening—   who now
                succumbs to the
frack-coaxed quake?

We survey
        our empire
        of inflict—

tally each blow

Mercury Lurks in My Milk Chocolate

now toxin avoidance diet, no histamines
or immune excitors, no toxic suitors
osteocytes ignite and hips swell

put a needle in to dye them, I am
advanced degeneration I am lead and
BPA-laced, VOC's erase stasis

sages say sip untainted everything, as if carcinogens
weren't already sown everywhere, who cares
to find unleaded air, land nourished and nourishing

endless forage, found in the mythical marsh
our harshness, that which brings us to suckle poison
these prisons of unpalatable bromines and selenium

blind hum of hostile elements, the sacrament
of transaction, look around to see batteries spilling
looking like hands holding long dead

oil-slicked fish, a sick pink drenched in rot
like advanced degeneration, what generation doesn't
slough venom, sanctioned into them, the nuisance siphoned off

into claims of no fault, fault us, hips falter, clean-food altar
glyphosate serves up hives, served in polystyrene, sirens
silent, business as usual, the usual visual, this Anthropocene fester-feast

beast of bullseye, last chance to not hit 2 degrees, last chance
to stem the tide, to tidy the body, take this cortisone shot, metal pierces
epithelium and in the interim, cue the containment, the panacea, pangea-pure

I Heard Seawater is Blood Kin

Blood is mostly water, like the sea. Lakes are mostly water, like the sea. Water is not blood, blood is not the sea, and we have no idea how to quench this dissonance.

Seawater is a complex mixture of 96.5 percent water, 2.5 percent salts, and smaller amounts of other substances, including dissolved inorganic and organic materials, particulates, and a few atmospheric gases.

Sometimes the watery eye of the universe fixes and holds like the first third eye, impassive yet curious, noticeably noticing, peering, assessing, watching, yoked, as if the eye could perceive all yet might initiate a finite number of interactions per iteration of intention, as consciousness can be so intricate, and oceanic, and with such vast linkages, that to fix just one sea stare would be folly, yet to see all would be a shallow skew, salt-stained and submarine, cobalt battling grey-cerulean blue for exclusive refractive hue, seawater swept, dissolved, daughtered.

The six most abundant ions of seawater are chloride (Cl^-), sodium (Na^+), sulfate ($SO^2{}_4{}^-$), magnesium (Mg^{2+}), calcium (Ca^{2+}), and potassium (K^+), making up about 99 percent of all sea salts.

A bit of blue-green sea glass, cast off and carved smooth, abraded into siliceous softness, caressed, coveted, humming the exact hue of seawater, as only blue-green wavelengths penetrate, and as blue-green light is most available for scattering, and as the sea is blue-green only to our eyes, yet the true hue of water is an intrinsic property from selective absorption and scattering of light, caressed and coveted, sea glass blue-green, humming hues the exact blue-green softness of smooth.

Other major dissolved substances of seawater are inorganic carbon, bromide, boron, strontium, and fluoride.

There is a reward for untainted water, for H_2O free of microplastics, pure, lacking poly(ethylene) poly(propylene), and poly(styrene). Yet we wasted our ransom. Thin voices lurk like priests in protest.

Concentrations tilt and taint in great stints, seawater stains, rivers of air whisk the tintiest of plastic particles from port to patch, from gentlemen to gyres, our waste windborne, copious, weeping saline. Thin wet protests for taint lurking, water ransomed.

Other constituents of great importance to the ocean's biogeochemistry include inorganic phosphorus (HPO_4^{2-} and PO_4^3) and inorganic nitrogen (NO_3^-, NO_2^-, and NH_4^+), constituents, those being essential for growth of marine life.

Everything that breathes, understands the importance of water. Everything that lives, understands the importance of metabolism. Everything that is made of atoms, understands the importance of electrons. Everything that everythings, understands. Importance.

The processes that deliver dissolved, particulate, and gaseous materials to the oceans ensure that they contain, at some concentration, very nearly every element that is found in Earth's crust and atmosphere.

Everything in all things. Broken linkages, come clean. Every all breaks every. Linkages, clean break. Everything breaking, all things linking. Come clean. Every clean linkage comes broken. Everything in all things. Every broken linkage, cleaned. All broken things in everything. Come.

In oceans, at depth, salinity alters. In fissures, water carry salts. Salts dissolve from rock fires and ferrous oozes, become hot with ions, burn with electron fervor and atomic suchness. In oceans, at depth, salinity alters if seawater percolates into deep-ocean volcanic fissures. Seawater returns to the greater ocean superheated, carrying salts from the earth's core into our acid trash oceans, at depth, altered.

Now there are 5.25 trillion (5,250,000,000,000) macro and micro pieces of plastic in our oceans and 46,000 pieces in every square mile of ocean, weighing up to 269,000 tons. Every day we add around 8 million (8,000,000) plastic pieces of taint. Five point two five trillion pieces to come clean.

Look at This Bliss

Look, don't turn your back on these mountains, don orange-sun
mountain dandelion, this agoseris, thoughts like plagioclase,
an earnest nest, sung by prairie remnants, was memory, how we crush
this innocence, incensed by earth's gashes, gnashing reserves from
sustainability swift-swerves, blessed essence, this revery eyes carry
from grief and gasp, look at this bliss, this heart-heavy agoseris, us.

Acknowledgements

"Nor Could the Sun" *Terrain.org*, March 2022 (poem and video poem).

"Knowing is a kind of prayer" *My Core Rises: Mycorrhiza Collection, Plants and Poetry,* April 2022.

"Be Still, Mere Molecule" *Arboreal*, May 2023.

"Mercury Lurks in My Milk Chocolate" *The Calendula Review*, November 2023.

"Wood Parade" in *Tupelo Press* anthology *The Last Milkweed,* February 2025.

"I hear how calendula petals" *The Whitefish Review,* Summer/Fall 2024.

"There Will Be Harmonies", "Foraging Behavior of the Wood-rotting Fungus" and part of "Marginalia on The Table of Elements Including Names, Symbols, and Atomic Numbers" *Science Communication,* July 2024.

"April 17, 2023, 48.498337°, -114.437207°" and "Why Not Inhabit Sunlight?" *Plant-Human Quarterly,* October 2024.

Notes

Scientific literature informs some of my work. References are provided in one reference list and here by poem. For each of these poems, some language, concepts, and/or information was incorporated from the respective source(s).

"And In This Regard We Breathe Shapes"

Kim, Taejoon, et al. "Therapeutic Potential of Volatile Terpenes and Terpenoids from Forests for Inflammatory Diseases." *International Journal of Molecular Sciences*, vol. 21, no. 6, 2020, p. 2187.

"Comprehensive Natural Products II: Chemistry and Biology, Volumes 1–10." *Journal of the American Chemical Society*, vol. 132, no. 28, 2010, p. 9929.

"Ensnaring The Pain Burden"

Dubner, R, and M Gold. "The Neurobiology of Pain." *Proceedings of the National Academy of Sciences - PNAS*, vol. 96, no. 14, 1999, pp. 7627–7630.

Raffaeli, William, and Elisa Arnaudo. "Pain as a disease: an overview." *Journal of Pain Research,* vol. 10 2003-2008. 21 Aug. 2017, doi:10.2147/JPR.S138864

Turk, Dennis C, et al. "Treatment of Chronic Non-Cancer Pain." *The Lancet (British Edition),* vol. 377, no. 9784, 2011, pp. 2226–2235.

Zeidan, Fadel, and David R Vago. "Mindfulness meditation-based pain relief: a mechanistic account." *Annals of the New York Academy of Sciences* vol. 1373, no. 1, 2016, pp. 114-27. doi:10.1111/nyas.13153

"Foraging Behavior of the Wood-rotting Fungus"

Fukasawa, Yu, and Koji Kaga. "Timing of Resource Addition Affects the Migration Behavior of Wood Decomposer Fungal Mycelia." *Journal of Fungi* (Basel), vol. 7, no. 8, 2021, p. 654. https://doi.org/10.3390/jof7080654 (note: Yu Fukasawa granted permission to use this image)

Sheldrake, Merlin. Entangled Life: How Fungi Make Our Worlds, Change Our Minds & Shape Our Futures. First US ed., 2020.

"Gneiss of the Cascades Core or O Orogenesis"

Zuluaga C., Carlos A, and Harold H Stowell. "Multidisciplinary Approach to Study Migmatites: Origin and Tectonic History of the Nason Ridge Migmatitic Gneiss, Wenatchee Block, Cascades Crystalline Core, WA, USA." *Earth Sciences Research Journal*, vol. 12, no. 2, 2008, pp. 235–264.

"How We See Photons' Slight Glimmer"

Gaurab Karki "Physiology of vision." Online Biology Notes. Jan 18, 2018, accessed Mar 3, 2022. https://www.onlinebiologynotes.com/physiology-of-vision/

Kolb, H. "How the Retina Works: Much of the Construction of an Image Takes Place in the Retina Itself through the Use of Specialized Neural Circuits." *American Scientist*, vol. 91, no. 1, 2003, pp. 28–35.

"I Heard Seawater is Blood Kin"

Kedzierski, Mikaël, et al. "Chemical Composition of Microplastics Floating on the Surface of the Mediterranean Sea." *Marine Pollution Bulletin*, vol. 174, 2022, p. 113284.

Byrne, Robert Howard, Mackenzie, Fred T. and Duxbury, Alyn C.. "Seawater." Encyclopedia Britannica, 5 Nov. 2020, https://www.britannica.com/science/seawater.

"It would be just like you, universe"

Hardinger, Steven A. 2017. "Chlorophyll" from "*Illustrated Glossary of Organic Chemistry*" http://www.chem.ucla.edu/~harding/IGOC/C/chlorophyll.html

"Mother of Pearl, or One of the Manifestations"

Lin, Albert, and Marc André Meyers. "Growth and Structure in Abalone Shell." *Materials Science & Engineering. A, Structural Materials: Properties, Microstructure and Processing*, vol. 390, no. 1, 2005, pp. 27–41.

"Ramping Up"

Andrews, Robin George. "Solar Storm Destroys 40 New SpaceX Satellites in Orbit." *New York Times (Online)*, 2022, New York Times (Online), 2022-02-09.

"Show How It Might Be So"

McTaggart, Lynne. *The Field: The Quest for the Secret Force of the Universe.* 1st ed., HarperCollins, 2002.

"There Will Be Harmonies"

Zhang, Jieyi, and Francisco M Vargas. "A Novel Approach for the Prediction of Viscosity of Water Alkanediols Mixtures." *Fluid Phase Equilibria*, vol. 479, 2019, pp. 63–68.

"Two Fungal Species Among Many Play Telephone and Ferret Food"

Beiler, Kevin J, et al. "Architecture of the Wood-Wide Web: *Rhizopogon* Spp. Genets Link Multiple Douglas-Fir Cohorts." *The New Phytologist*, vol. 185, no. 2, 2010, pp. 543–553.

References

Andrews, Robin George. "Solar Storm Destroys 40 New SpaceX Satellites in Orbit." *New York Times (Online)*, 2022, pp. *New York Times* (Online), 2022–02–09.

Beiler, Kevin J, et al. "Architecture of the Wood-Wide Web: Rhizopogon Spp. Genets Link Multiple Douglas-Fir Cohorts." *The New Phytologist*, vol. 185, no. 2, 2010, pp. 543–553.

Byrne, Robert Howard , Mackenzie, Fred T. and Duxbury, Alyn C. "seawater". *Encyclopedia Britannica*, 5 Nov. 2020, https://www.britannica.com/science/seawater. Accessed 20 March 2022.

"Comprehensive Natural Products II: Chemistry and Biology, Volumes 1–10." *Journal of the American Chemical Society*, vol. 132, no. 28, 2010, p. 9929.

Dubner, R., and M. Gold. "The Neurobiology of Pain." *Proceedings of the National Academy of Sciences - PNAS*, vol. 96, no. 14, 1999, pp. 7627–7630.

Fukasawa, Yu, and Koji Kaga. "Timing of Resource Addition Affects the Migration Behavior of Wood Decomposer Fungal Mycelia." *Journal of Fungi (Basel)*, vol. 7, no. 8, 2021, p. 654.

Hardinger, Steven A. "Chlorophyll" from *"Illustrated Glossary of Organic Chemistry."* 2017. http://www.chem.ucla.edu/~harding/IGOC/C/chlorophyll.html

Karki, Gaurab "Physiology of vision." Online Biology Notes. Jan 18, 2018, accessed Mar 3, 2022. https://www.onlinebiologynotes.com/physiology-of-vision/

Kedzierski, Mikaël, et al. "Chemical Composition of Microplastics Floating on the Surface of the Mediterranean Sea." *Marine Pollution Bulletin*, vol. 174, 2022, p. 113284.

Kim, Taejoon, et al. "Therapeutic Potential of Volatile Terpenes and Terpenoids from Forests for Inflammatory Diseases." *International Journal of Molecular Sciences*, vol. 21, no. 6, 2020, p. 2187.

Kolb, H. "How the Retina Works: Much of the Construction of an Image Takes Place in the Retina Itself through the Use of Specialized Neural Circuits." *American Scientist*, vol. 91, no. 1, 2003, pp. 28–35.

Lin, Albert, and Marc André Meyers. "Growth and Structure in Abalone Shell." *Materials Science & Engineering. A, Structural Materials: Properties, Microstructure and Processing*, vol. 390, no. 1, 2005, pp. 27–41.

McTaggart, Lynne. *The Field: The Quest for the Secret Force of the Universe.* 1st ed., Harper Collins, 2002.

Raffaeli, William, and Elisa Arnaudo. "Pain as a disease: an overview." *Journal of Pain Research* vol. 10 2003-2008. 21 Aug. 2017, doi:10.2147/JPR.S138864

Sheldrake, Merlin. *Entangled Life: How Fungi Make Our Worlds, Change Our Minds & Shape Our Futures*. First US ed., 2020.

Turk, Dennis C, Prof, et al. "Treatment of Chronic Non-Cancer Pain." *The Lancet (British Edition)*, vol. 377, no. 9784, 2011, pp. 2226–2235.

Zeidan, Fadel, and David R Vago. "Mindfulness meditation-based pain relief: a mechanistic account." *Annals of the New York Academy of Sciences* vol. 1373, 1, 2016, pp. 114-127. doi:10.1111/nyas.13153

Zhang, Jieyi, and Francisco M Vargas. "A Novel Approach for the Prediction of Viscosity of Water Alkanediols Mixtures." *Fluid Phase Equilibria*, vol. 479, 2019, pp. 63–68.

Zuluaga C., Carlos A, and Harold H Stowell. "Multidisciplinary Approach to Study Migmatites: Origin and Tectonic History of the Nason Ridge Migmatitic Gneiss, Wenatchee Block, Cascades Crystalline Core, WA, USA." *Earth Sciences Research Journal*, vol. 12, no. 2, 2008, pp. 235–264.

ABOUT THE AUTHOR

Rebecca A. Durham is a poet, botanist, and visual artist. She is the author of the award-winning ecopoetry books *Half-life of Empathy* and *Loss/Less*. Durham holds an undergraduate degree in Biology, master's degrees in Botany and Creative Writing, and an Interdisciplinary PhD. She has worked across the west as a botanist and ecologist, with over twenty years in western Montana where she lives with her daughter. Find more of her work at rebeccadurham.net.

www.ingramcontent.com/pod-product-compliance
Lightning Source LLC
Chambersburg PA
CBHW041144120626
46547CB00020B/3108